Key Ballah

Key Ballah

Copyright © 2015 Key Ballah

All rights reserved.

ISBN: 1515130517
ISBN-13: 9781515130512

To my Father,
who gave me this skin,
and this life.


And to
God,
who gave me my father.

Key Ballah

It has taken me years to write these poems.
For so long they were too stuck in my throat.
But now,
they are here,
and they hurt,
and I love them.

Key Ballah

Skin & Sun

Bismillah.

Skin & Sun

Key Ballah

Today is for the Women.

I am a woman,
who was born of a woman,
who was born of a woman.
He is man,
who was born of a woman,
who was born of a woman.
We are both
only water, heartbreak,
and a trembling fear of God,
like our mothers,
and their mothers.
Still he speaks of his limbs
as if he were Adam(as),
who was the only man
who did not come
from a woman.
Who will explain to him
that his miracle
is his mother.
His mother.
His mother.
His mother.
Three times
his mother

**I grieve my sisters**
lost to wars
they did not wish to fight.

**You are only the bare bones of a woman,**
the bare beautiful bones.
Everything else is just experience,
mixed with blood.

For My Alien Girls,
Thank you for being extraterrestrials.
For showing me the multiplicity of blackness,
of brownness,
of girlhood.
For showing me that women can be strange
and beautiful
and odd
and beautiful
and brilliant
and beautiful.
For showing me that identity is complex,
not single minded.
For reminding me that being unique in my identity is
okay.
For giving me the courage to write my truths
for making me feel that it is okay
to be from another planet.
For telling me that even my peculiarity
is worthy of love.

Thank you.

—— ps. Thank you mama Badu, for being weird and black and
amazing, you've saved me often.

**I was a child when
I became a woman.**
A thing I do not wish
upon any bewildered child,
who's body
is ready,
too soon before her heart.

**They do not know**
the kinds of women
they create
when they touch at night,
or in the day,
or at school,
or on the playground,
or in a closet,
or in the pool,
or in the backseat of a car.

The way that they turn
little girls
in
to
foul mouthed women,
with hooks
for hands
and spines
for tongues.

If they only knew
the kind of women we've become,
because of the way
their hands found us,
when we weren't old enough to know better,
they would cut away their own hands
in disgust.

**I am the product of centuries of women**
who have learned to tend to their own backs,
with  their own oiled hands
and  their own split black knuckles
and their own yellow palms.

I am from a line of women
who have evolved mouths that slow kiss honey
even after
a full body burn.

I am from the blood of women
who's eyes are always kind
even after
witnessing
their homes
break
into a bloody war dance,
a home,
attempting time and time again
to swallow them whole.

I was grown out of the bones of women
who birthed armies from blood,
and plucked love,
straight from the hands of God.

Who is more resilient than us,
flowers that grew
straight from the mouth of the devil.

You come,
two moons on your chest
sun in your skin,
God in your hips.

**I see why they fear you
when you are the full sky.**

Say to yourself: an affirmation

I am wealth of body
I am wealth of flesh
I am wealth of beauty
I am wealth of history
I am wealth of human
I am wealth of bone
I am wealth of worthy
I am wealth of passion
I am wealth of ability
I am wealth of deserving

**We grew to be women**
who could fill our bellies with oceans,
who could fill our skin with sun,
but refused to fill our hearts with love.

It is too difficult to be vulnerable,
it was only yesterday
when we began to truly understand what we are worth.

You ask
if I like to play with fire.

You say that I always smell like someone's home,
burning,
and burning,
and burning.

That I smell like
memories,
photos,
kitchen table conversations,
forgiveness standing in the threshold of the bathroom,
screaming matches in the living room in front of the tv,
I love yous sent as peace offerings across the dark space
of the bed.

You say I smell like losing this.
That morbid sweetness that the masochist feels,
that reluctant relief that comes when everything is
burning.

You say that I am the tangible manifestation of a history
on fire.

You say,
          "you don't just smell like sadness,
          you smell like the kind of sad that seers
childhood out of paint"

And I can only rub my skin and say,
I am a woman who has outlived many homes,
**I can't always tell when I am burning.**

**Self Love To Do List:**

1. Always remember my worth.

2. Never forget to prinioties myself first.

3. Be content

4.

5.

6.

7.

8.

9.

10.

I am beautiful,
especially when I'm angry.
When there are no words,
and I am my purest form of rage.
They tell us that women
should cry quietly,
and birth our anger in secret.

But I
will rain over everything near,
unforgivingly loud,
**my beauty**
**is in my angry rebellion.**

I carry tragedy
like a designer bag,

I am learned in the art of dressing up disaster
making it look like a bridesmaid,
who is more beautiful than the bride.

My Grandmother taught me
how to paint the face of bad news
so that it doesn't make you look too old.

**I have seen women make their pain
look like the Garden of Eden.**

**Because
women are supposed to be pretty and soft.**
But what if we are soft and not pretty,
or pretty but not soft.

What if we are neither.

What kind of women are we then?

**They tell us,**
that as women,
we should feel embarrassed if we are alone.
But sometimes,
as women,
alone is a place we go,
to feel empowered.

**To the women who**
aren't soft around the edges,
dainty on their feet,
delicate in their hands.
To the women who cannot be called
Rose, or Lilly or Petal.
To the women who
are full bodied
and wide hipped.
Gripping their parts,
pulling and pressing trying to fit
themselves into a single mouthful.

**Stop.**

There is no one way to be a woman

**To the women in my life**,
you are water.
I need you,
and I am made up
almost entirely of you.

Momma
Aunty Nuha
Cree
Khadija
Aunt Stacey
Granny
Nanny
Aunty Schazelle
Rochelle
Sarah
Magda
Aunty Susie
Tyauna
Rochelle
Edil Ayan
Kiru
Hibaq
Iris
Arij

**Women are water,**
because men are taught
they must
be stone.

**My grandmother's hands are rough.**
I hold them tight in my soft hands and feel shame,
my carefully manicured fingers look haunting beside her
calloused aching hands.
She says that her hands are the result of pine sol, dirty
floors, and motherhood.
I kiss apologies into them.
I hold them to my soft lips,
and breath good memories into them
hoping they are softened by nostalgia.
She says it is the price of being a woman,
and I
am sorry for that.

**In war**
it is us
the women
who bleed most.

**I was magnificently undone by her,**
she had the intensity of 1000 dying stars.
Bursting at the seams with galaxies and darkness.
There was nothing about her that I did not love.
There was nothing about her
that did not make the world around me softer,
and better,
and brighter.

But this world does not know what to do
with women who love each other.

**Remember when you touched me?**
and you said, this is the way that men touch women
when they are in love.

When you left and I was alone,
I felt the new breasts growing on my chest,
and wondered if it was these that made me a woman.
I looked at the new hair that was sprouting between my
legs,
and wondered if it was this that made me a woman.
I looked at my little girl body in the mirror,
this body that was whispering into the ear of adult,
I looked at it and I wondered
what kind of eyes you had
to see a woman.

**This is for the women.**
The distant Women,
the Women with home on their breath.
For the haphazard Women,
the distrusting Women,
the flighty and cautious,
both emotionally attached and unattached Women.
The Women who have been hurt too many times,
the too smart to be abandoned again Women.
The pulled apart Women
the perpetually looking for a fresh start Women.
The Women who lie through their teeth,
and their eyes
and their hands,
because the truth is too terrifying to admit.
The Women who stand on train platforms
willing themselves to jump.
The Women with children who sometimes wish they
didn't
but are too ashamed to admit it.
To the Women who's bodies are soft and full.
To the women who cover everything but their eyes
to the women who cover nothing but their eyes.
To the women with God
and to the ones who are not.

I wrote this for you,
and for me,
and for us.

So that you may know
that you are not alone in your truths,
even the ones that hurt to admit.

**I am transient in my existence.**
Somedays I manifest in all of the space around me,
closing my mouth over every honest space.

Other days I'm not so sure that I exist at all.
This, is the nature of being both woman and human and
black simultaneously.

Today is for the self.

Your body
is the truest place
you will ever travel to.

You should grieve
every word lost
when you violently
try to quiet yourself.

Self policing
the amount of space you take up
because you are a woman,
or black,
or brown,
or fat,
is an act of self destruction.

You should know,
that the universe is ever expanding
so that we can fill out more and more space as we grow.

**Do not allow the universe to expand and then not be
filled out by your greatness**,
because that
my love,
is one of the greatest acts of injustice.

**The truth is:**

I'm not all the way there with the self love,
but I swear to God,
I'm trying.

At the end of the day
I undress.
I take the day off of my shoulders,
unclip the love from my back,
spread it out on the bed,
and lay down in it.

**We have to remember to be gentle with ourselves**,
to say "Today I will love this part right here,
because yesterday it was hard for me."

Key Ballah

Sometimes,
it feels
as though
I am a sheep
parading myself
in the clothing of a wolf.

**My body has never left me.**
But I cannot count all of the ways in which I have left it.

I was ashamed
of skin
and hair
and bones
that belonged to my Mothers,
and their Mothers
and their Mothers.

I am an incarnation of grandmothers past.
This body and it's history have never left me,
even though I continuously choose to leave it.

You tell your body to keep quiet.
To fit nicely into spaces, tidy, neat, clean and kept.

But you are abundance
made out of flesh.
An abounding being
fashioned from goodness.
and goodness
and goodness.

Instead of living cramped inside of yourself,
spread yourself out like a field,
let your soft parts tell you how they came to be so
tender.
Treat their words as a lesson
because when this whole world is hard and bloody,
it takes love to
keep you soft
and light.

Remember.
Remember.

we are indeed
spiritual beings
having a
human experience.
Say ;

I **AM** the soul
I **HAVE** the body.

Sometimes I can run my fingers across my bare skin
and know exactly how every wound came to be here.

Other times this land feels so unfamiliar
that I am tempted to stop at every corner and ask,
"How do I get back home ?"

Today **I am not a collection of soft stories**
nor a garden of love.
I am a metropolis of memories,
I am ancient,
ancient,
ancient,
a city polluted by the past,
a woman lighting herself on fire,
only to build herself
back up again.

I am no phoenix
I am a woman.

Understand,
i am only **wilderness** wearing skin
an entire continent of blood.

**I am soft**,
in more ways than one.
And there is no shame
in the quiet revolution
that comes from
letting yourself
settle into your own skin
and saying
"This is not a place I've always loved,
but I'm learning and I'm trying"

Peace.

**There are moons inside of you.**
Full and throbbing.

**I have called the new moon home.**
And she came willingly,
she wept in my doorway
but could not enter.

She said she'd forgotten what kindness looked liked.
"It's been years,
years, since I let myself find rest and be vulnerable."

And I know this too,
it's true,
too many years of darkness
can take its toll on the soul.

**Reach across the hurt.**
You are there,
waiting for yourself.

**Say this:**

I am more than my
productivity.
I am more than my
productivity.
I am more than my
productivity.
I am more than my
productivity.
I am more than my
productivity.
I am more than my
productivity.
I am more than my
productivity.
I am more than my
productivity.
I am more than my
productivity.
I am more than my
productivity.
I am more than my
productivity.
I am more than my
productivity.
I am more than my
productivity.

I am more than my
productivity.
I am more than my
productivity.
I am more than my
productivity.
I am more than my
productivity.
I am more than my
productivity.
I am more than my
productivity.
I am more than my
productivity.
I am more than my
productivity.
I am more than my
productivity.
I am more than my
productivity.
I am more than my
productivity.
I am more than my
productivity.
I am more than my
productivity.

Breath.

Breath.

**Sometimes,**
I search and search my whole self,
often finding nothing
but sadness.

Sometimes,
it takes everything I am
to convince myself
that light lives here.

**I am currently**
learning to heal through
kindness,
it is proving to be
the greatest test
of my character

When people say;

*"God never gives you more than you can bare."*

I know

that those people

have never had to bare

the weight,

of being touched by a man

who they haven't invited into their bodies.

Everyday
I return to myself.
I come home
to my body,
to my skin,
to my God,

and I say,

*" Man, what a world this is,*
*I am so grateful for you."*

Meet God in the sacredness of loving *you.*
*Fully.*

**1.**      Your goodness is wide open
like sprawling body
begging flesh,
like delivering moon
swallowing Caribbean Sea.

2.      Your kindness is becoming.
It makes you beautiful.

3.      You are water to my eyes.

4.      Tear away the partition,
there should be no intercession.

5.      You are an embodiment of Gods intention,
teaching us how to need.

**Your father could have been kinder**,
he could have been gentler,
he could have held his tongue
and his fists.
For some of us he could have stayed,
for some of us he should have left,
for many of us it might have saved us if he told us that
he loved us.

But despite him,
despite all of the times you felt yourself choking on hate
for him,
despite the fear that still rattles your bones,
you are who you are despite of him.

You survived.
You learned to love
to tend
and mend,
to be kind,
to be gentle,
to breathe.

As cliché as this sounds,
Forgiveness really is for you.

Today is for the Revolution.

Self love is a revolution,
especially for women of colour.
When everything in this world tells you that you're not
enough,
believing that you are is incredibly revolutionary.
Do not let someone else's privilege convince you that
you are not amazing and brave and inciting change
through the act of loving who you are.
Perhaps in a perfect world there would be no need for
revolution like this,
but when my nine year old cousin is asking to lighten
her skin,
even not finding yourself repulsive is a victory.
Maybe for some people the colour of their skin doesn't
make self love a personal revolution,
but every morning that I wake up not hating my body
is a moment in time when I celebrate the end of a life
long war.
How can liberating your own body,
not be revolutionary?

I swore myself away to be someone I wasn't,
disappeared myself into memories
and wore skin that was too light to be mine.
Pressed the kink out of my words, and my hair.
Folded my tongue in on it self to speak a language that
wasn't meant for people with mouths like mine.

We are the products of colonization
Alhamdulillah though,
our stories don't end there.

I am a consistent cloud
of heavy rain
and anger
and love.

A storm
perpetually brewing  in the chest,
a life always on the cusp of revolution.

I am
I am
**I am.**

The stories that refugee children have to tell with their
bodies
is a deafening one.
It is a dying  scream running out of a burning home.
It is gun powder on the breath.
It is rot in the skin.
It is boarders made out of limbs.
It is civil wars that aren't really civil wars.
It is mass graves disguising themselves as sink holes.
It is peeling away eyes and nose and ears but leaving
mouth.
It is feet that have had to memorize their way away from
death.
It is contorting to fit into freezers and boxes, trunks and
ships.
It is suffocating and abandoned in the back of a truck on
the side of a highway.
It is the casual nature of loss.
It is not understanding how you, or your parents, or your
siblings, factor into to the broken politics of a country
that was once so beautiful but now a pile of rocks.
It is somewhere in the third world wondering if you are
even in the same galaxy as the first.
It is watching your parents give away their life savings
only to capsize three km away from the promise land.
It is the creeping barrage of occupation.
It is women who can't swim, but in chaotic desperation

throw themselves and their babies into an ocean, hoping

that somehow, (perhaps by the grace of God), they will

make it to shore.

It is always forgetting about refugees with black skin.

**The stories that refugee children have to tell with
their bodies is a deafening one.**

Why is there  more empathy for lions named after
colonists,
than there is for driftwood made out of children?

— **For the babies lost at sea.**

When my father is
out in the world,
he speaks
cautiously.
One word
after the other
arranged neatly into
sentences
that do not leave red marks
seared on  top of
translucent hands.
But inside his body
he is brewing with anger.
Deep seething
ruining anger.
Forget a storm
he is the universe
folding in on it self.
He is heaven
at war with hell.

He is the final trumpet.
He is fire beating own its
chest.
He is a man who has been
silenced
who has been shamed
who's anger
has been erased from
history books
Who's ancestors
are locked within the
cage of his chest.
Who's skin speaks before
him.
Who works twice as hard
to reap half as much.
I often wonder how,
this beautiful, gentle, soft
spoken man
is still capable of kindness
when this world has made
men like him
imploding stars.

We are not people who fear the sun.
Light is truth
and we
are ready.


**Melanin**

Ask yourself :


Who am I without my colonized self?
Who am I without my oppressor?

These are questions that make me sick,
because these are questions I cannot answer.

Dear language that I will never know,
forgive me for writing all of my poetry in english.


Dear Mother tongue that I will never learn,
forgive my tongue for not remembering all of her
mothers.
she weeps for all of the love she'll never know.


Dear Grandfather that I have lost,
I pray the continents together,
so that one day I may walk home to you.

**I write stories**
using my Mother's blood
and my father's name.
My ancestors are lined up
in my mouth
waiting for their chance speak.

Some of the worst **violence** I have ever experienced,
has come to me
from the mouths of lovers,
has come to me
at the hands of academia.

A lynch mob
could not do
the damage
that those two have done to me.

To be a child of the
diaspora
means to live haunted
between home that does
not want you and home
that does not belong to
you.
It is to be the star
in a tale of vagabondry
that is often not romantic
at all.
It is roaming too many
worlds but always being a
stranger.
It is the tragedy of
ambiguity, of having to
convince everyone that
you belong somewhere,
even when you don't know
where that somewhere is.
It is to always be on the
edge of rupturing from
dizziness.
It is to make a map of your
body.
It is to sit at home
at a kitchen table
at 3 o'clock in the
morning, with tea, and
cousins and uncles, who
want to hold a match to
the dirty politikkk$ and
dictator$$$hip that

plagues your mothers
throat, whilst
knowing you have no
place in the struggle
behind her teeth or the
revolution happening in
her belly.
You've been away from
her breast for too long,
you cannot speak to her
like you are her child.
It is to watch home
asphyxiate slowly,
stone cold hands crushing
black esophagus
It is watching home
unravel at the seams whilst
being fisted by greed and
only being able to hold a
damp rag to her forehead
while she dies.
It is to say that you are of
a people and wonder with
bitter sadness if they
would ever say that they
are of you.

Being a child of the
diaspora is to say the word
home and always hear  in
its place,
the word imposter.

There seems to be an intense
disparity in the lifespan
of black/brown childhood.

In this body
where there is war
my skin
my hair
my language
fight to leave me everyday
and everyday
I love them back into themselves.
**The processes of fighting
to keep yourself together
is truly exhausting.**

In these streets
where there is war
bullets collide
with black skin,
spilling black blood
into black earth.
And at the end of the day we are all enveloped into a
black sky.


But still you wonder where you came from?

On this earth
where there is war,
a sadistic thirst for profit,
is
the
cause
of it.

The stories of love,
aren't always beautiful,
aren't always useful,
aren't always light.
Especially when you are talking
about home.
Those stories are often
a gnashing of teeth,
a busting of limbs,
fire upon fire,
skin upon skin,
mother upon daughter,
father upon friend.
I've heard that the Tower
of Babel was made
entirely out of
immigrant limbs.

When I have sons
I will teach them,
how to play dead in the street.
I will show them
how to lay on their backs,
with eyes so vacant
the stars will come down out of the sky
and try to make a home in them .

They will learn how to make their skin as cold
as the concrete they are spilling over,
and their father will teach them how to hold their
fingers,
so that their hands aren't mistaken for guns.

It is the only way I can think of to keep them alive,
teaching my sons to play dead when everything around
me tells me they already are.

Key Ballah

I love my father's laughter,
and his skin
and the way that he hides home in the corners of his
mouth.

He lives in a world that is afraid of him.
That cowers beneath the potential
hidden in the cracks of his skin.

A world
who out of fear of his greatness
tells him to be small

but he chooses
everyday
to love big.

What a gift he is.

Colonialism is <u>always</u> a trigger.

## To My Sons I will say,

You can be soft and beautiful.
I will say,
they will try to steal every bit
of tenderness from your skin.
I will say,
hold your gentle close.
I will say,
they will try
to rip your humanity away from you
but hold it close,
it is yours
there is nothing more yours than that.

It's quite a thing
to be a collection of oceans,
forced to believe
you are only a mouth full
of spit.

Some days
you are spread apart
in every direction.
**Pulled apart**
**by trauma**
and trauma
and trauma,
compounded
and cemented,
building upon itself,
until it is a weight
that sits in your chest,
most days it is not easy to love yourself,
and some days it is not easy to persuade yourself to live.

When the colonizer bleeds
we all go running,
apologies ready
on the breath.

All the while
our homes are burning
but no one comes running for us.

**They destroy your country,**
with their guns,
their bombs,
their drones,
their men.

And then turn around
and shame you
for trying to escape their disaster.

This. is. how. to. oppress.

**I have had to hold together continents with my full body,**
because I am always two places at once.
Two separate ends of a sphere,
ironically,
never feeling whole.

Key Ballah

**How do you**
kiss your mother
with the same mouth
you use
to shame women who look like her ?

In Vincy,
where the caribbean sun kisses the sand,
and the soles of our feet know what walking really feels
like.
Where our ancestors kissed each other,
and loved each other,
and fought each other.

Where they came when they
survived the journey across big watah.

The small island
that holds big secrets
and big stories
and big love.

Where my father almost drowned after big rains,
and got the scar on his knee from falling out of a big tree
.
Where he climbed coconut trees
and stole donkeys from a neighbour's backyard.

Where thick skin is how you survive,
where we laugh at all of the ways we've had to survive,
where my grandmother met my grandfather,
where my great grand parents died,
where time goes backwards and forwards
the island of my life.

Dear Caribbean Sun,

Thank you for being so kind to my people.
I know it is hard to see what this world has done to us,
but we speak many tongues and we use many tools.
Survival was built into our skin.

**Your melanin isn't quiet.**
It was born with a wide mouth,
full lips,
and a throat that has had to learn
how to swallow back oceans.

Please do not quiet your skin,
do not suck it in
or pin it down,
it's too beautiful to be silenced.

Never  forget that your mother
made you
from the stretching
and destruction of her own body.

And
blood
and
blood
and
blood
and
trauma
and
love.

See how talented she is.
See how she built your bones
out of air and hurt
and oceans,
that she crossed to be here.

Out of her rage,
you were born
And out of her rage,
you were loved,
and that
is an impossible task.

**They said**
"perhaps,
If You straightened Your hair,
You would be more palatable.

Perhaps,
Your skin would seem less strange.

Perhaps,
if You looked a bit more like us
and we could learn to trust You"

Why do they always think
that We were made
to fit into their mouths?

When I'm here,
I call there
"back home"
and people nod,
they understand that
I am here occupying this
space,
but that it is not my true
space,
not my real space.
They understand that I
belong somewhere else
somewhere where I am
more fluid,
more myself.
Somewhere where my
name is familiar and my
skin is at home .
Somewhere where they
look at my nose and say
"Ah, you are the daughter
of so and so"
Somewhere where they
hear my name
they smile and tell me how
they knew my
grandfathers.

But when I'm there,
"back home",
they ask me how long I
will be staying,
when
I will be going
back home.
They make the food
milder,
the tea sweeter,
they slow the roll of their
tongues and wash out their
accents,
they call me american girl,
British girl, foreign girl.
They laugh at the way my
skin peels when the sun is
unforgiving,
the way that I eat mangos,
and how much chicken I
leave on the bone.
And I remember,
that I am an inbetweener
always straddling two
selves, two continents, two
worlds,
never belonging
completely
anywhere.

Sometimes with all of the love I have in me
and with all of the hate you have in you,
I wonder how we can stand under the same sun,
how we were made by the same God.

It is uncanny
what guilt can do to the body,
what fear can do to the mind.

— to the woman who spat at me on the metro

I take inventory of my
lover's limbs before he
walks out of the door.
The honey warm,
sandalwood of his skin
both excites and breaks
my heart.
He kisses me on my lips
before he leaves and says,
I'll come back to you
soon.
I take a mental image of
everything he is wearing, I
look at the time on the
stove, I draw a mental map
of his route, I estimate the
steps from door to door.
I recall the genuine
intention in his voice when
he promised to return.
I replay it.
I dissect it.
It was there,
I am certain.
He has always been a man
of his word.
My sister calls and tells
me they shot another black
boy.
I ask her where her son is,
her voice cracks over the
word "school".
We both say "inshaAllah"
at the same time.
If God wills it.
If God wills it, he isn't
laying somewhere dead in
the street for four and a
half hours.
If God wills it, he isn't
being choked to death
telling unhearing ears he
can't breathe.
If God wills it, he wasn't
mistaken for one of his
brothers today.
If God wills it, he was not
shot in the back in a train
station.
If God wills it, he kept the
orange tab on his toy gun.
If God wills it, he left his
toy sword at home.
If God wills it, he keeps
his hands out of his
pockets.
If God wills it, he doesn't
eat a chocolate bar, or
reach for his wallet, or
walk down the street, or
play his music too loud, or
wear a hoodie, or carry a
back pack, or wear his
pants too low.
But that was too hard to
say,
so we both simply said
inshaAllah,
because in place of all of
that,
it was the only thing that
made sense.

1. some days i miss him so bad i want to rip my hair out.
2. it often feels as though i'm too heavy for love. who do you know that even their ghosts have baggage?
3. you manipulated me, and i let you. perhaps it is because i was tired of starting over.
4. i try to be so many people at once. but they are all destroying each other.
5. is perpetual loneliness hereditary?
6. i'd honestly prefer the sticks and stones, over the words... words have always hurt me.
7. it is exhausting being so angry, but admittedly, it is the anger that keeps me alive.
8. when i was young i used to pull out strands of hair, hoping straight hair would grow in it's place.
9. we were too afraid to be alone, that is why we couldn't leave. even while we destroyed each other.
10. you said that you loved me too soon and i felt obliged to say it in return. i know too well what it is like to be emptied by unrequited love, i think it was only that we ran out of things to say.

— **10 things you hoped you'd never have to admit**

Today is for the love that couldn't last.

It was always this,
a choice,
a fork in the road
a decision calling to me
a child in your eyes that begs me not to go
a child that promises he'll be good this time,
a child that swears he'll behave
and I
am in the habit of choosing that child
every time,
of always choosing you,
every time
But today
the revolution
is simply this:
From now on
I'm choosing myself
every
time.

And
here
we were.
left.
undercut by love
current dragging
us violently by our hair
and God
reaches out a hand
to touch the water
and there and then
it is still.
but when i
bring my hands to it
i bring catastrophe home.

**In the part of your legs**
where the dessert begins,
he said he would come back to you
but you are still waiting.

Dry mouthed men have come for their chance to squeeze
themselves into you,
into your vastness.
thirsty
thirsty
thirsty.
But you hold your self at the same length that he left you
in, waiting for him to return
so that you can pick up
exactly where you left off.

There is no space for men who come,
no oasis turned body for them to burn through,
no limbs for them to kiss and leave wanting.

You lay waiting for him,
it has been too many months
and I know that
you are growing tired of swallowing moon,
you
are
getting
hungry.

He, had his mothers eyes
and his fathers mouth.
His smile stretched over
years of my stagnant
dreams.
He, heavy with what could
have been, was aching
rivers when we met.
And I, young and
innocuous, was bleeding
an ocean of affirmations,
trying to forget how
exhausting surviving water
can be.
His beautiful face wore
pieces of my personal sun,
rising and setting with his
every breath.
I, enamoured and in love
waded into him waist
deep, coddling moon
between my hips, and fire
in my lungs.
He, earth toned and
brilliant waved into
existence galaxies with his
hands as he spoke.
I watched planets shoot
from his fingers while he
commented on Socrates'
delusion and Mansa
Musa's power,
I was renewed by him,
and with him.
He was my calendar,
years began and ended
with his eyelashes rising
and falling,

months came and went
with the expanding and
contracting of his chest.
Days were only decided
by the length of time
between each I love you.
He was a history of love
unto himself.
And I, a major in his
biology and a minor in the
mathematics of his
existence, undid myself in
studious enrapture of his
being.
See if I were to still keep
time by his watch,
I would tell you that I
loved him forever.
But now that I have
returned to reality,
now that my sky isn't a
reflection of the colour of
his skin,
and my days aren't
measured by his steady
midnight breathing,
I will tell you that I loved
him for a day that felt like
forever,
for an hour that felt like
eternity,
for years that that felt like
years too long.
Because loving him was
beautiful,
but washing myself away
to love him was not.

Give.
Hug your bones.
Pour water over your hair.
Rub all of the distilled love out of your skin.
Say
"this is a new body,
a place he's never been"
Say it again.
And again.
Now spread it out,
with your full tongue,
with your mouth like your mothers,
with your teeth like your grandmothers .
Those women know the art of silent suffering,
of regrowing their skin,
of braiding the cold out of their hair.
Let the words of renewal penetrate deep.
"He has never stepped foot into this place,
this new place you've become.
He has not poured this water over his hands,
he would not recognize it,
this place would scare him,
he does not deserve to tread here,
even with bare feet"
Let them touch you softer than finger tips,
let them leave the bruise of
"I was hurting before
but God is Kind
and I am healing"

Have you ever seen a flower
wither into nothing?
They say God is in the details,
but **bitterness can eat its way
through anything.**

**Today I am tired**.
More tired than yesterday.
More angry than
yesterday.
Deserted and worn.
I am so many things in one
home,
I've been known to hoard
bodies but give them no
names.
My bed is always warm,
and it is exhausting.
Peel your eyes away from
your lids,
and see me flashing,
I am your homing beacon.
Your face, a star on my lit
path to heaven.
Your mouth, a place in
which I have learned give
birth.
I knew, when I met you,
that you would be my test
on this earth.
And women in my family
are hardly ever wrong.
When my cousin
suspected her husband was
leaving,
she saw him laying in the
neighbours yard in a
dream.
When my aunt found out
that my uncle was going to
die,
she dreamt that her bed
was cut in two and his side
was burning.
When my grandmother
told me that she knew that
her husband would be
heavy handed, she had a
dream that he had
bouquets of flowers
instead of fists.
I had a dream last night,
that you called me from
the centre of an empty
room and I was standing
right beside you.
You called and called and
called but you did not see
me near you, or feel me
touching you.
"Come home" I said, and
you went.
"Come home" I said, and
you went.
"Come home" I said, and
you left.
*I am my mother's*
*daughter.*
*I am my mother's*
*daughter.*
*I am my mother's*
*daughter...*

You broke my heart
and
I lived.

**I was drawn in**
by an opportunity to love you
but even as time passes,
I am still thirsty for blood.

I know that I am a beast of a woman.
and I know you were hoping for sheep.

Key Ballah

I want to cry all of the time
for all of the ways you could not
hold me
and love me.
For all of the times I closed my mouth
when I should have said something
hoping that if I was silent
I wouldn't scare you away.

Among all the places on my body where there is war,
the place where you live has been the most violent.

**We are a couple of lovers,**
fighting for breath.
Making ourselves sick trying to love each other.
You are no good for me,
I see every lie you tell
float to the top of your skin,
but still I smile
and wrap my mouth around you,
trying to soften you.
And you,
you need a woman who is far less needy,
far less demanding,
and I don't know how to be any less than I already am.
But we
(Like many lonely lovers do),
still cram full our bellies
with all of each other.
Telling ourselves that it is better to be full to the brim
with a charred loneliness parading itself as love,
than starving,
and burning with vacancy.

**I am almost done**
cutting it all away,
everything that I grew
to be what you wanted.
Everything I said
to make you feel safe,
it all got over grown
after you left,
and I
was lost in the mess of it.

But I am almost done,
you are almost gone,
I am almost
free.

**I wrote poems
about you**.
And after all of these years,
I often wonder
how thoroughly
my hands embellished
your kindness.

I have begun to wear God
**too close to my spine.**
And I am glad,
because that means
there is no longer a place for you.

**We just**
never got the timing right.

Or at least
that's what I tell myself,

to live with the fact,
that perhaps
you simply
did not want me.

**Sometimes,**
You wait for love your entire life,
and then one day someone comes along
and hands you something and calls it love,
but you know better
even if
they do not.

What a powerful man he
is.

**I was
the most beautiful place
he'd ever known.**

Look at
what he can do.
With a only few months
and only a few words.

Now,
I am a ruin.

One man,
bringing an entire city to
dust.

He returns to me
sometimes when the moon
is full,
to take photos,
smiling,
amidst the atrophy.

One man,
bringing a whole woman
into disrepair.

And when he surveys his
devastation,
he is proud of what he's
done.

He comes some nights,
to sink his teeth into the
relic
that I have become,
but he never stays long,
he knows
I am haunted.

I fell out of myself
trying to love you,
and I can't figure out
how to put myself back.

Praise God
who came too late to save me
but right on time
for what I deserved.

By Allah,
I would have swam across days for you.
Now I go days
without thinking of you
at all.

I was an open and shut case.
I was in love
but not loved,
an irrefutable tragedy.

Read through your conversation once more before you
delete it. Count how many times (s)he says"I"
and the amount of times (s)he says "you".

Note the difference.
Let this be the last time you let (her) him tell you that
(s)he loves you , and let (her) him lie to you in the same
breath.

What a waste it was
to have written poetry
about you.

I will never understand,
how I put my full body
in the mouth of a man,
and expected him not to use his teeth.

I cannot continue to come away from myself to love

you,

or write about you.

I am not
a mourning person
but your absence
is like the silent still blackness
that comes home at 3am .

**Do you ever wonder
what it would be like
to have me?**
To wake up next
to poetry spilling
out of your bed.
To be written into
stories where
as ordinary as you are,
even the sun rotates
around you.

He creates the space.


And then asks…

"why you so distant?"

I often wonder
if being in love
ruined the poetry.

**Do not move yourself over to love someone else.**
Stand still and say
"This is me,
I am many things
but most of all,
I am at home in this body."

After that,
the rest of your journey
making yourself believe
that
that is true.

Today is for the love that made you a home.

This lover of mine,
is unaware of how much I love him,
is unaware of the flowers growing out of my back
for him,
it is always for him.

I am a field of congratulations for him,
a parade of applause for his existence,
a walking acknowledgement
of what too much love can do to a woman.

**Dear lover,**
with the beautiful mouth
and the pensive eyes,
and the hands
that I have imagined
a million times
resting gently
on the small of my back
or in my hair
or on my hips
or in my mouth.
I pray for you
and your mother
and your father
and your sisters
and your brother
and your hands.
I pray for you
try to understand how much I love you,
when sometimes I pray for you
and forget to pray for myself.

**I would cut this city in half for you.**
Unhinge all of the hanging lamps in the sky for you,
bring them here for you,
make them into a canopy to hang over our bed for you,
kiss all of my sweetness into your mouth,
handpick all of the goodness I can carry and feed it to
you,
steal silver away from the moon and give it to you as a
dowry.

For you,
I'd do it for you.
For you,
for you,
for you.

**I did not wake up**
bright and in love with you,
but you said my name once
and it sounded like forever.

**Sext:** We listen to Blackstar, Tribe, Fela, Bob and Barrington Levy, while you talk about your personal commitment to deconstructing systematic racist patriarchy, while simultaneously rubbing homemade Shea butter whip into my hair. Whilst I, read to you, poetry from my mother's books, we eat fried plantain that was cooked low and slow. You say lets take a nap, in the middle of a cloudy day, we lay down in warm white sheets, your body pushed up against mine, but not "pushed up" against mine, you really meant what you said when you said "let's take a nap".

When we wake up you say "it's been 50 years since an unarmed black person was killed by the police", you say "the Congo is safe and thriving off of her own natural resources", you say that "West Indians have saved themselves from neocolonialism masquerading as tourism", you say "the trauma of dictatorship is finally able to heal", you say "the prison system has been abolished", you say "they have agreed to give us our reparations", you say "Africa is coming back to herself", you say "there is no more occupation", you say "sea levels are returning to normal", you say "child workers have been liberated", you say "there is no more war in shams", you say "there is no more poverty", you say "there is no tax on feminine hygiene products", you say "we have busted the lens of the colonized eye", you say "we have found the key to unchain our colonized minds", you say "I bought you a house with a pool, on land that isn't stolen", you say "people aren't being forced to drink polluted water", you say "you no longer have to be afraid walking home alone at night", you say "big brother died", "you say they've found the perfect balance between democracy and socialism", you say "your ends are so moisturized!", you say "we have learned the importance of community", you say "our history is taught all year round in school", you say "human dignity is valued", you say "humanity is restored", you say "cultural appropriation is a thing of the past", you say "capitalism has breathed its last breath" you say "love is the key", you say "love is the key", you say "love is the key", you say you say "let me take care of you", you say "lay back let's celebrate finally being free".

**There are edges of you**
that I have not travelled to.
I only see them in the distance
and hesitate to make the journey.
I am afraid to cross over
the beautiful,
the tender
and the still,
only to find myself in a place
that I cannot learn to love.

**I wake**
**to everything that you are**,
I am full
and you are
spilling over the sides of me,
my cup is running over.
This body
a shell
that sews me desperately to the seams of this earth.
This vessel is undeserving
of a love so big.
It has
stretched outside of me,
the skies weep
at their inability
to hold such a beautiful thing,
as we approach the ceiling of this life,
we are praying for surety of the next.
You say
"there is too much love here,
I am drowning in it"
I say
"Let heaven be it's container then"

**What does love look like?**
It's every emotion you've ever felt,
Stretching out and nestling in.
It's today and tomorrow.
It's yesterday. It's mercy.
It goodness. It's uneasy.
It's loud. It's quiet.
It's hurt. It's forgiveness.
It's exciting. It's surprising.
It's heavy. It's light.
It literal and figurative.
It's coming. It's going.
It's still. It's moving.
It's laughing and crying.
It's open. It's closed.
It's in the bones and on the skin,
and in the hair and on the lips.
It's with God, It's with you.
It's angry, and calm.
And right and wrong.
It's wonderful and beautiful
And scary and overwhelming
and over time and all at once.
It's empty and full.
It's everything you are,
everything you were,
everything you will be.

To admit to love,
is to completely sever
every and any hold
you have over
yourself.
It is to say,
I trust you with
every part of me.
It is to say,
here,
I have faith
that you will
take what you
need and
still leave me full.

It is to say,
my life is yours
and God's.
It is to say,
I came wholly
from your rib.
It is so say,
I leave my breaths
on your name
and send them to
the eternal garden.
It is to say,
I am your country.
It is to say,
lay your burdens
here.
It is to say,
khalas,
it was written.

The sun,
tip toed
through our long curtains,
and cast her long fingers
along the perfect angles of your beautiful face.
She was gentle with you,
in ways I could only hope to be.
She,
hummed warmth in soft whispers quietly to my skin,

She said
"Be kind to yourself,
this is love,
**it has to be."**

**Bring**
Bring your
good
quite
love here.
Sometimes this life gets too loud
and I ache for a quite place to rest,
to retire,
to unpack.
Sometimes,
I feel like I could sit still for a hundred years.
Sometimes,
I want to sleep for ten. full. decades.
But when you
bring home your good love,
I am renewed in every moment
and rest
is suddenly unnecessary.

Do you remember the day,
when we sat in your
Mother's kitchen
while her curry bubbled on
the stove, and her rice that
smelled of coconuts boiled
in the pot ?
Do you remember how she
danced around the kitchen
on the tips of her toes to
music from back home, a
country that I had never
been to, but had seen,
many times,
traced deeply into your
bare back and again traced
delicately, at the base of
your neck.
Your Mother in her
english, (her english that
sounded like it had been
dipped in earth) her
english that said, I am
many things, I come from
many places, the kind of
english that does not let
you forget your ancestors.
The kind of english that
makes room for home,
the kind that lets your
people sing with you,
in chorus, in the body of
your song.
Your ancestors were there
flowering from her mouth
dancing with her in that
kitchen,

holding you both in their
hands.
I watched her grab you by
the waist and pull you into
her.
Her hips swayed to the
music like it was made for
her, and yours, yours
swayed like they were
made for me. Sun
streaming through
windows kissing your
mothers bare arms, the
hair on her arms smoothed
softly to one side. I wanted
to kiss both of your eyes
and the one that helps you
see all of the things that I
never could. I remember
you that day, how you took
up the whole room,
the garlic on your mother's
hands,
the pepper on her breath,
and you,
you filled the air
and I took you in, every
lingering bit of you.
It did not last
but I will always be
grateful to you for that
moment,
when everything was
right, and God was in the
room.

You were incredible,
wrapped in the brilliant glow of morning.

Eyelashes stretching across generations
fluttering love into the fill of my stomach.

My arms asked for you by name,
and my heart asked for you by flowering out of dry soil,
your water helped me grow.

Your love helped me become.

The afternoon sun was warm,
it felt like melting cinnamon against my skin.
The rays danced on your cheekbones
turning you into a gold dipped statue.
I watched the sky burst with love
and spill pastels into the atmosphere.
Just over your head,
I watched through the loop holes of your curls,
your laughter pull stars into the sky.
You rolled onto your side in the cushion of the grass
and kissed my cheek and my neck,
your lips felt like warm honey.
I wrapped my arms around you
whispering to you that this felt perfect,
that I was scared of things that felt perfect,
that I had the tendency to distrust things that felt too
good.
But you cupped my face in your hands,
brought your lips close to mine,
and said,
that good things felt good,
and bad things felt bad
and that you had never known anything to be perfect.

Except us,
Except now,
Except this.

My heart
has been
waiting
to love you
for so long.
And now
you are here,
and I am ready.

To me
You feel like
those moments after Fajr when anything is possible.
Like crawling into bed after a disastrous day.
Like driving through the city at night in the rain.
Like the warmth of a bonfire.
Like hearing something so beautiful it sends shivers up
your back.
Like a midnight in August when the air is sticky and
your night has just begun.
Like kissing my mothers hands.
Like gratitude finally coming home to fill me out.
To me,
You feel like perfect cups of tea,
and days when you've accomplished every goal you've
set for yourself.
Like my favourite song on repeat.
Like seeing my father pleased.
You feel like a place I can finally stretch out.
Like the mouth of heaven,
opening wide,
saying
"Finally, you've come home."

I've spent years
not knowing men to be kind.
But you came
with the softness of a trillion
purple skies and the quiet
of overcast with a chance of rain,
and you showed me,
that some men
do not know how to be
anything but.

You will breathe
gentle stories into my neck,
kneed decades of loss out of my back,
untuck the universe from my waist,
and kiss new galaxies and dimensions into my mouth.
We will bring the tide in.
We will relieve the moon so that she may rest.
We will watch over the night tangled into one another
like vines wandering away from tree, curious and
wanting.
You will turn my name from something that waits,
to something that is anticipated.
Let our jaws lock in gratitude to our Lord.
Let our bones crack in worship.
And if we must drown,
let us do so in an ocean of thanks.

Do his words make you feel like
you deserve a piece of the sky
cut out and sewn with soft gratitude into your back.
Do his hands make you feel like
you are worth a lifetime of sadness
finally returning home and setting itself free.
Does he try to understand you,
your quiet,
your apprehension.
Does he step carefully into your water and say
"I am committed infinitely to your vision.
Infinitely to you."
When he peels away your misery and your shame,
is he embarrassed by the way you are flowering
unwaveringly beneath.
Does he hold you with the palms of his whole hands
or only with the tips of his fingers.
Does he say "I love you"
with the entirety of his body,
or is it just sweltering echo from his inner thigh.
Do you sleep well beside him,
or are your dreams still lonely and lost.
Could you stay there,
could you unpack.
When he says "forever."
does it still make you feverish?

There are men,
there have always been men,
who wrestle their own egos to own space in women like
me.
Flighty women,
who watch themselves passing in mirrors,
who lay awake at night and count the longing within
them.
Who choose to spend time with themselves in quiet
thought,
who prefer their own hands.
Women who can't remember the last time they've
washed themselves in salted rivers,
women who can't remember ever being in love.
Those men want to conquer.
They want to bleed us.
They want to look at the space that she occupies and say
"there,
that is mine too."
But you,
You fill me out differently.
You fit into me in ways that don't require me to sign
over the deeds to myself.
You say
you are yours
and I am mine
and we belong beautifully to each other.
This morning,
I woke with your breath on my lips,
your arms around my waist,
I smelt you in my hair,
even with oceans between us
you still exist where you belong.

Sometimes Allah's signs
don't come in the form of grand epiphanies.
Sometimes you don't wake up in the middle of the night
pouring out of a dream clear and sure.
Sometimes the sign comes in the form of a prayer,
where you are praying for his forgiveness as wholly as
you are praying for your own.
Where your hands are shaking as your
prayer turns the entirety of your body into an earthquake,
partly out of fear of your God and
partly out of gratitude to him that
He has finally given you someone
that can make your heart feel

Key Ballah

Go away now,
and love yourself.

Key Ballah

اللَّهُمَّ إِنِّي أَعُوذُ بِكَ مِنْ الْهَمِّ وَالْحُزْنِ وَالْعَجْزِ وَالْكَسَلِ وَالْبُخْلِ وَالْجُبْنِ وَضَلَعِ الدَّيْنِ وَغَلَبَةِ الرِّجَالِ

Allahumma inni a'udhu bika minal-hammi wal-Ḥuzni wal-'ajazi wal-kasli wal-bu<u>kh</u>li wal-jubni wa ḍalaEid-dayni wa <u>gh</u>alabatir-rijal

O Allah, I take refuge in You from anxiety and sorrow, weakness and laziness, miserliness and cowardice, the burden of debts and **from being overpowered by men.**

Key Ballah

CPSIA information can be obtained
at www.ICGtesting.com
Printed in the USA
LVOW04s1829240416

485103LV00030B/974/P